Mountain

by Laura Hamilton Waxman

BELLWETHER MEDIA • MINNEAPOLIS, MN

Note to Librarians, Teachers, and Parents:

Blastoff! Readers are carefully developed by literacy experts and combine standards-based content with developmentally appropriate text.

Level 1 provides the most support through repetition of high-frequency words, light text, predictable sentence patterns, and strong visual support.

Level 2 offers early readers a bit more challenge through varied simple sentences, increased text load, and less repetition of high-frequency words.

Level 3 advances early-fluent readers toward fluency through increased text and concept load, less reliance on visuals, longer sentences, and more literary language.

Level 4 builds reading stamina by providing more text per page, increased use of punctuation, greater variation in sentence patterns, and increasingly challenging vocabulary.

Level 5 encourages children to move from "learning to read" to "reading to learn" by providing even more text, varied writing styles, and less familiar topics.

Whichever book is right for your reader, Blastoff! Readers are the perfect books to build confidence and encourage a love of reading that will last a lifetime!

This edition first published in 2016 by Bellwether Media, Inc.
No part of this publication may be reproduced in whole or in part without written permission of the publisher. For information regarding permission, write to Bellwether Media, Inc., Attention: Permissions Department, 6012 Blue Circle Dr., Minnetonka, MN 55343.

Library of Congress Cataloging-in-Publication Data
Names: Waxman, Laura Hamilton.
Title: Life on a Mountain / by Laura Hamilton Waxman.
Description: Minneapolis, MN : Bellwether Media, Inc., 2016. | Series:
  Blastoff! Readers: Biomes Alive! | Includes bibliographical references and
  index.
Identifiers: LCCN 2015033099 | ISBN: 978-1-62617-319-4 (hardcover : alk. paper)
                                ISBN: 978-1-62617-517-4 (paperback : alk. paper)
Subjects: LCSH: Mountains–Juvenile literature. | Mountain ecology–Juvenile
  literature.
Classification: LCC GB512 .W38 2016 | DDC 577.5/3–dc23
LC record available at http://lccn.loc.gov/2015033099

Table of Contents

The Mountain Biome

Julian Alps, Slovenia

One of Earth's **biomes** is found higher up than any other! It is the mountain, or **alpine**, biome.

It begins above the **tree line**. Its snowy peaks are some of the planet's **harshest** places.

Himalayas, Pakistan

The alpine biome exists thousands of feet above **sea level**. Mountains that reach great heights are found across the globe.

highest peak on continent = ▲

mountains = ⬜

Denali
(Mt. McKinley)
20,308 ft (6,190 m)

Mt. Elbrus
18,481 ft (5,633

equator

Mt. Kilimanja
19,340 ft (5,895 m

Aconcagua
22,835 ft (6,960 m)

Vinson Massif
16,066 ft (4,897 m)

The world's tallest mountain is Mount Everest in Asia. It rises over 29,000 feet (8,840 meters) high!

N
W · E
S

Mt. Everest
△ 29,035 ft (8,850 m)

Mt. Kosciuszko △
7,313 ft (2,229 m)

Mount Everest

The Climate

Bernese Alps,
Switzerland

The mountaintop **climate** is known for temperatures far below **freezing**. But the extreme cold does not last all year at lower heights.

Temperatures can reach 60 degrees Fahrenheit (16 degrees Celsius) just below the peak. Other biomes exist closer to the bottom.

Mountain Zones

Alpine:
11,500 feet (3,500 meters) +

Subalpine:
10,000-11,500 feet (3,000-3,500 meters)

Montane:
8,000-10,000 feet (2,400-3,000 meters)

Foothills:
6,000-8,000 feet (1,800-2,400 meters)

Plains:
4,000-6,000 feet (1,200-1,800 meters)

The temperature drops 3.5 °F (2 °C)
for every 1,000 feet (300 meters) gained.

Sea level: 0 feet (0 meters)   Heights listed for Colorado's Rocky Mountains.

Mountaintops are dry, windy places. Only about 12 inches (30 centimeters) of rain or snow falls each year.

Himalayas, Nepal

The snow on the tallest
mountain peaks does not melt.
It stays frozen all year.

Rockies,
Canada

conifers

Just below the tree line are tall **conifers**. These trees cannot survive higher up.

Most alpine plants are small and low to the ground. This keeps the icy wind from blowing them over.

mountain bearberry

dwarf birch and blueberry

Alpine plants are able to grow in dry, rocky soil. Their leaves and stems soak up wetness from the air. Flowering plants bloom during the warmer growing season.

alpine gold

alpenrose

Low levels of **carbon dioxide** cause plants to grow slowly.

alpine ibex

Little **oxygen** in mountain air makes breathing hard. Many alpine animals have big lungs.

Thick fur and extra fat keep most alpine **mammals** warm. Some animals change color with the seasons. This is for **camouflage**.

white-tailed ptarmigan

Himalayan tahr

Some alpine animals **migrate** in winter. They move down mountains for warmth and better food.

mountain goats

snow
leopard

Other animals **hibernate** during the coldest months. But the toughest animals are active all year long!

Mount Everest

Location: Asia; Nepal and Tibet

Height: 29,035 feet (8,850 meters); tallest mountain in the world

Temperature:

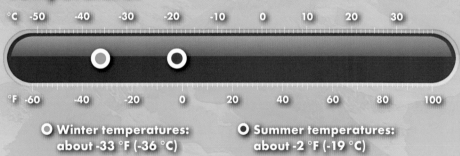

○ Winter temperatures: about -33 °F (-36 °C)

○ Summer temperatures: about -2 °F (-19 °C)

Precipitation: 18 inches (46 centimeters) per year

MOUNT EVEREST FOOD WEB

snow leopard

Himalayan tahr

bharal

Himalayan vulture

alpine grasses

yak

Other important plants: rhododendrons, mosses, lichens; no plants grow near the peak of Mount Everest.

Other important animals: red pandas, Himalayan black bears

Glossary

alpine—related to the tops of tall mountains

biomes—nature communities defined by their climate, land features, and living things

camouflage—a way of using color to blend in with surroundings

carbon dioxide—a gas in the air that plants need in order to grow and survive

climate—the specific weather conditions for an area

conifers—trees that usually have needlelike leaves that stay green all year long

freezing—32 degrees Fahrenheit (0 degrees Celsius); the temperature at which water freezes into ice.

harshest—the most extreme and unpleasant

hibernate—to sleep or rest through the winter

mammals—warm-blooded animals that have backbones and feed their young milk

migrate—to travel from one place to another, often with the seasons

oxygen—a gas in the air that animals need to breathe; air has less oxygen at greater heights above sea level.

sea level—the height of the sea's surface

tree line—the highest point on a mountain where trees are able to grow

To Learn More

AT THE LIBRARY

Callery, Sean. *Mountain*. New York, N.Y.: Kingfisher, 2012.

Ganeri, Anita. *Exploring Mountains*. Chicago, Ill.: Heinemann Library, 2014.

Kalman, Bobbie. *Where on Earth Are Mountains?* New York, N.Y.: Crabtree Publishing Company, 2014.

ON THE WEB

Learning more about mountains is as easy as 1, 2, 3.

1. Go to www.factsurfer.com.

2. Enter "mountains" into the search box.

3. Click the "Surf" button and you will see a list of related web sites.

With factsurfer.com, finding more information is just a click away.

Index

The images in this book are reproduced through the courtesy of: Natalia Pushchina, front cover (mountain goat); Perspectives-Jeff Smith, front cover (hawk); Dan Breckwoldt, front cover (background); DeepGreen, p. 4; Tommy Heinrich/ National Geographic Creative/ Corbis, p. 5; Daniel Prudek, p. 7; R.Babakin, p. 8; Bellwether Media/ JE illustration, p. 9; Bartosz Hadyniak, pp. 10-11; Sandra Cunningham, p. 12; Scandphoto, p. 13 (top); Gregory A. Pozhvanov, p. 13 (bottom); Tom Grundy, p. 14; Inu, p. 15; michelangeloop, p. 16; Robert E. Barber/ Alamy, p. 17 (left); Alexandr Junek Imaging s.r.o., p. 17 (right); ra-photos, p. 18; Jeannette Katzir Photog, p. 19; Keith Taylor/ Alamy, p. 20; Dennis W. Donohue, p. 21 (snow leopard); tristan tan, p. 21 (Himalayan vulture); mariakraynova, p. 21 (yak); Dmitri Gomon, p. 21 (bharal); Dennis Jacobsen, p. 21 (Himalayan tahr); Pavel Ilyukhin, p. 21 (alpine grasses).

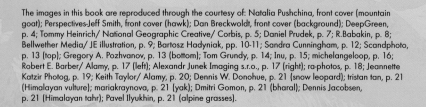